My Mind
My Heart
My Soul

My Mind
My Heart
My Soul

Yolanda Harrison

G Publishing, LLC
Detroit, Michigan

My Mind, My Heart, My Soul

Published by G Publishing, LLC
P. O. Box 24374
Detroit, MI 48224

ISBN: 0-9776780-3-2

Printed in the United States of America

Dedication

This book is dedicated to Lisa "Leevis" Shelton, and her four children, William, Wrandell, Wanee, and Aushanai. Due to your untimely death in 2004, I know you can't be here with me in the physical, but I know you will always be here spiritually. Lisa, you said in your book that I inspired you, but I always felt that you were the strong one. And, I just want you to know that *"Those Chics Inc."* will live forever. I promise to do everything possible to make both our dreams of writing come true.

Love forever,
La-La

Acknowledgments

I would like to thank God for His grace and mercy throughout my life. To my childhood sweetheart and husband DeAndre Wilson, and our wonderful children, India, Chelsea, DeAndre Jr., and Kobe Wilson. To my mom, Wanda Faye Jones, you are my best friend and I love you dearly. To my father, Willie C. Browner, who is no longer with me, thanks for never giving up on me. To my second father, Tom Jones Jr., thanks for being there for me. I love you. To the best aunt in the world, Aunt Daisy, thanks for treating me like one of your own. To my grandmother Mary and grand-daddy Arvie, thanks for remembering to call me on my birthday. To my sister and brother, Tonya and Kenneth Harrison, even though our lives are taking us in different directions, I still love you both. To my Georgia boys, Patrick, Paul and Andres Browner, thank you for being great big brothers. To my Aunt Lisa (Mya) thanks for being the successful woman that you are. To my cousins Shay, Chase and Neanna, love you guys. To my in-laws, Bruce Wilson, thanks for being there for me. To Latricia Browner and family, thanks for all the kindness you showed me after the death of my father. To Robin, thanks for the late night talks. To Page, Sabrina, Armont, Nyesha, Sean, Tadarian, and Tyann, thanks for putting up with me all these years. To Darrell, know that my love for you will always be. To Mary Tooles, who encouraged me with her own writing. To Ms. Mikki, thanks for pushing me to continue to write. To Veronica, thanks for the pep talks and prayers. To Tyronda, thanks for all the info and encouragement, and to LaShanda thanks for getting me out the house to party!

I would like to thank all my aunts, uncles and cousins: Lil Queshawn, Mariah, Jazz, Pancake (Andrew), Diamond, and Angel; my nieces and nephews: Narada, Paul II, Joshua, Safira, Satira, Mikey, and Boonie, Chloe "Bell", Little Kenny, DeShawn, Mama D, Devin, Duke, Re, Donovan Lamone, Deon, AuJanee, Dasia, Ashley, Jasmine, Destiny Raven, Rayanna, Zariah, LaChina, Diamond, Lakayla, and Little Fred.

To my childhood best friend Celestial Adams of D.C. and her family. Finally, to my extended family: Lisa, Gary, Boobie, Pete, Dre, and Tyesha. To my new son Greg and the Detroit Titan Pal football team. To Joyce Gowdy for coming to my poetry reading. To Re-Re, Wheezy, Derrick, Davion, Dasia, Peanut, Salena, Samantha, Martisha, J-dog, Brenda, and Sam. To Sheila, Shay, Ronnie, you were there for me when I needed you. To Domonique, who inspired me to write One Mother, and her unborn child. To E-40 and family, Ced, Boo, Deion, and Al Bal and family. To my hairdresser, Larry and family over at Dejavu Hair Salon. To Kim, Domonique, Whitney, for your great spiritual friendship. To R.T. for your friendship and encouragement. To my street family: Heady (Lee) for watching over us all these years, I don't think I would be married if it was not for you driving us to Ohio, much love. To A.D, love you little brother. To Biggie, Ralo, K.D., K.O., Po, D-boy, D-bo, Big Juan, Turtle,Cease, Smeets, Little Cookie, Tone, Chris (Micheal Jackson), Fatso, Curtis and family, and to my uncle Clue. To Uncle Quincy, Sponge Bob, C. J., Mr. Love, Mrs. Legs and family, Mr. Jesse, Mrs. Pearl, arissa, Juanita and family, and to Ben Ross Academy in Warren. To Rudy, Tone, Melissa, Michelle and family, Drea, S, and Cry Baby. To all the fellas on the Dover and Keating, and to anyone whose name that I did not mention, much love to all.

Special Thanks

I would like to send a special thank-you to Writers for Christ Christian writing group which I am a member of. To the members: Minister Renita Willis and family, you started an awesome club. Minister Theresa Bates, I got courage through you publishing your book. Sister Beverly, thank you for the nutritional guide. Sister KaJuana, thank you for your prayers. Elder Brown, thank you for your wisdom and prayers. And to the wonderful sister Willette Hayden, God sent you tom me at the right time. If I had not stepped out on faith and joined the group, I truly believe it would have taken me a lot longer to get to this point in my life and for that I thank all of you. To Pastor Mary L. Jennings, at Jesus Christ Apostolic Church, thank you for being a woman of integrity. You truly are a blessing. To my pastor, Pastor Ray Johnson and First Lady Leola Johnson and the Faith Reconciliation Tabernacle members, thank you for all the love and encouragement through my learning season. Last, but not least, to the greatest publisher in the world, Ms. Julia Hunter of G Publishing, LLC, thanks for being so patient and believing in my project, you and your staff are awesome.

Love,
Volanda

CONTENTS

NOTE TO THE READER

Love, relationships, family, friends and enemies and all of the joys and pains of everyday life experiences are expressed through the pages of this collection of poems, My Mind, My Heart, My Soul.

Every poem has a story behind it that may not necessarily be about me, but has been inspired by someone else's life journey. Being exposed to these everyday life experiences has in return, made me get to know myself better.

The time, effort, and strength that I put forth into the creation of this collection has truly brought forth my faith in Christ. I learned that being saved does not take away the worldly problems, but teaches you how to become humble, patient and learn to strengthen your faith as you go through the problems. I hope at least one of the poems in this book be a testimony for something that is going on in your life or someone you know and will help to uplift their spirit. So take some quiet time, get comfort-able, and enjoy.

MY MIND

Open up your mind to receive the gift of knowledge. For without it, do you really have an opinion of your own? Or do you have to depend upon someone else for one.

NO RHYTHM

I'm feeling you,
I'm needing you.
I'm loving you so much' as I try to groove to your
  smooth sounding beat.

I'm feeling you all down in my spine,
Flowing through my heart, and through my soul,
But for some unsound reason, I'm not feeling the
  same flow through my dancing feet.

You see,
Because I have no rhythm.

No control over the moves I make,
I'm loving you so much, that I don't care about my
  silly mistakes.
And knowing that you are my first love, not being
  able to hear you at all,
Would bring me such misery and heartache.

Because I have no rhythm.

When I hear you, I give in to your different
  attitudes, and styles.
Hearing you like for the first time, I begin to blast
  the radio,
Knowing I've been a lover of yours for sometime,
I begin to feel you all over again,
Waiting on you was worth my while.

You see,
Because I have no rhythm.

So as I make my way to the dance floor,
I don't care who's watching anymore.
I'll dance my groove all night long, cause each
    song I hear,
I'll be yelling,
"That's my song".

Even though'
I have no rhythm.

JUDGING ME

I'm choosing my words very carefully.
So that you may understand.
That I'm tired of you judging me,
Instead of accepting me for who I am.

I can't take away my illness.
If I could don't you think that I would?
Instead of taking all the pain from you
And simply being misunderstood?

I can only pray and learn to deal with it,
And you should do the same,
Instead you try to ignore it,
Or play the blame game.

So if you love me like you say you do,
Then you need to stop pretending nothing is
    wrong.
Just help me deal with it,
I need for you to be strong.

I'm no longer afraid of your harsh and
    intimidating words,
I've stood up and gotten the help that I need and
    deserve.
I want you to be part of my life, but I won't beg,
I hope that you one day educate yourself on the
    issue, and get it through your head.

I didn't choose to be bipolar; it was put upon me,
So don't you think it's time for you to grow up and
    stop ignoring me?
That's why I choose my words very carefully,
So that one day you can stop judging me.

A GIVING MOTHER

A mother gives, a mother takes,
A mother forgives, when her child makes
　　mistakes.
A mother accepts when her child sometimes do
　　things that puts her to shame.
A mother understands when her child's life seems
　　to be all screwed up,
And it's her you turn to and blame.
A mother is proud when you achieve things that
　　are great,
A mother silently cries alone when life gets hard
　　and she suffers constant heartbreak.
A mother comforts you, no matter what the
　　problem is,
A mother will give all she has until the very end.
A mother shares,
A mother loves,
A mother cares
A mother gives the greatest hugs
A mother is a mother
No matter what ever else she claims to be
A mother will be there always.
That's why my mother has always been a treasure
　　to me.

"I WONDER"

Do you think if I could sing like Jill Scott,
That my voice would be hotter than hot?

Or if I could dunk on the rim so high,
I would be just like Mike and fly?

If I was faster than Flo Jo, or threw punches like
Laila in the ring,

Could I get even close to being all that just being
me?

I wonder .....

"TEENAGE MOM"

My nose was wide open as some old folks use to
    say,
Would've done just about anything to make you
    look my way.
As soon as you did I thought to myself I would
    control the situation,
At that moment I thought I was grown, I just
    knew I could handle it.
Quickly I got a real dose of sinister lust, and my
    body didn't feel the same,
Over the next few weeks my hormones were flying
    all over the place,
I never had a clue that my life would forever be
    changed.
I kept it a secret for as long as I could,
But now that I think about it, it really didn't do
    me any good.
I got up the nerve to finally tell you,
And that was the end of the relationship to the
    boy that I thought I once knew.
It didn't take long but before my child came to the
    world and my baby daddy was gone.
Never taught no better, sex was kept a secret and
    never discussed,
As soon as it was a baby having her own baby,
All my parents could do was holler and cuss.
I didn't have any help, I had to grow up quick and
    learn to survive,

For my babies sake I had to learn to be a mom
without any lessons or guides.
As I look back now, I have no regrets but only to
have been much older and wiser when I
became a mother,
And for my baby to have had a chance to know her
father.

TRUE

Are you sure about the words that you say to me?
Are you sure that what you say is true and
    genuine?
Can you handle being up front and honest about
    who you are?
Because I need to know this before our friendship
    can even start
Now, make no mistake about it,
I plan to be as real and genuine to you as I can
I refuse to be no more and no less than true
No fakeness and no lies,
All I need is honesty or it'll be good-bye
So I need to know about the words that you say to
    me
Can I tell you my secrets and thoughts and what's
    really on my mind?
And not have to worry about my info spreading
    around town
Can I rely on you the way friends suppose to be?
Or will I have to always watch what I say around
    you
Cause your mouth gives out others people's busi-
    ness so freely
I need to know,
Are you sure about the words that you say to me?

IT HURTS

It hurts so much when someone you love,
Tell you that your dream is worthless
They tell you to let it go
Like a piece of paper blowing in the wind
Blowing so fiercely to nowhere
Because it has no end
Until the wind slowly becomes calm again
But by that time it's to late
The dream is lost
Forever
And you are just left standing there
Wondering could it have ever been

TEARS

Each tear
That
Falls
From my face
Represents
A story
That has
Taken place
In
My
Life
An everyday burden
After
Burden
Starts to build
Up about
To explode
Within me
Then the tears
Roll down faster and faster
Out of control
No more hold on it
I
Let go
To much baggage
To
Keep
Carrying around
These tears

Have to
Flow
Like a river
No end
No beginning
Just what it is
What
Life is
Right now
Giving me a tear
Many tears
Running
Down
My face

SELF- ESTEEM

Sometimes there are high and low points in our
lives

Every now and then it looks like nothing is going
right.

Learning to hold our heads up high at times, seem
so hard

Forgetting that we don't have to give up because
God is in our corner.

Everyday some type of negativity can easily break
our spirits

So easily we can give up and say this life is not
worth living.

Turn back to the assurance that God will not give
up on us

Ending all the self-doubt that continues to control
you.

Everyday wake-up with a new attitude of
believing

Meditating on God's word and put our faith first
as a task worth achieving.

WHAT I'M AFTER

What is it that I am after?
That would fulfill this empty space inside of me
Why my heart yearns while wanting to know why
    can't
A friend or family member love for me can't be a
    sure guarantee.
Why can't they love back, give a little more, and
    stop taking so much?
Can they not see through my eyes that I have
    suffered enough?
What does it take to get some of the goodness
    back?
Or am I being selfish?
No, probably not, but I sometimes feel so hopeless.
Giving is a gift and love is to,
But having the ability not to give and love is just
    so cruel.
So what is it that I am after?
True friends and family that can listen and judge
    not,
Just be there for me and be fair,
And when times get hard for me, not to quickly
    bail out.

WHY DID HE LOVE YOU THAT WAY

You say why did he love you with his fist
I respond by saying how did it ever even come to
    this
I mean
I was there
Right there
Missed all the signs
Now, as I sit here and reminisce
Could I have been so blind
The late night calls
Saying you've had enough
Never mentioning
That he had been getting so ruff
When I did notice some of the little things and
    mentioned them
You lashed back at me
By saying that I was just imagining it
Over the course of the years
You became a master
At covering up the bruises
Really
Really good
When I asked why you were still with him
You said he wasn't a bad guy
He was just simply misunderstood
When I finally got fed up
I was ready to explode
To put this lame in his place
You told me I had no right

That I should stay in a friends place
Several times after the fights
You said you were leaving
Again you fell for the I love you speech
That it would never happen again
Those lies is what convinced you to stay
I feel I failed you as a friend
Never was able to get you to understand
And see
That love shouldn't have to hurt
And a coward is what he is and always will be
Cause somehow we both should have known
That he never ever
Knew how to be a real man
And as I look at you lying in this hospital bed
About to die
All I keep asking myself is why did he love you
     this way?

I WANT OUT

I knew one day I was going to leave you,
You see, it was all along my destiny to
Cause I wanted out
All I ever dreamed of was being somewhere else
Somewhere different
Somewhere safe
Somewhere that love would show its' face
I wanted out
When I had to come back to you
I was in disbelief
Like I had been cut by a sharp edged knife
Or stricken by grief
You see,
Cause I wanted out
Having had a taste of pure satisfaction
Made me more and more distracted
Didn't realize what a responsibility it was to be
Somewhere new
So I slowly slid back down
To your level before I knew it
Even though,
I wanted out
I now see the many mistakes
I see now that much more was needed
I see that I needed much more discipline
Much more courage within me to achieve it
Because I still
Want out

SOMETIMES

Sometimes
You make it hard for me to love you
But yet, I manage to
Sometimes
You have your own way of hurting me
But yet, I choose to still be with you
Sometimes
You manage to piss me off
But yet, I've learned to still live with you
Sometimes
You push me to the point of wanting to walk right
    out the door
But yet, I stay because you promise not to do it
    anymore
Sometimes
You truly take my love for granted
But yet, I say nothing when I really should be
    more demanding
Sometimes
I can do nothing but smile at you and your
    screwed up ways
And those little things like that
Is what convinces me to continue to stay
Sometimes.......

I SHALL WRITE

I shall only write what I know
A mere experience of mine
Of what has happened in my life
That has gone and went by
Like a photograph the thought has been captured
Placed on an empty shelf unused until it is needed
    again
To be used to conjure up the memory
To be explored in my heart once more
And as I take the time to go over it in my mind
I bring forth its life just one more time

How could I dare to write about what I do not
    know?
For it would go unplanted like a flower
And the thought would not grow
It would only dry up and die
So as I go on through my life
I frame my experiences up high
For one day they might be used
I will put the thought together
And I shall begin to write
I will bring forth what I know
To continue to bring those memories back to life

MY HEART

To truly know and have
experienced love, is to truly know
and have experienced God.

WILL OF LOVE

To be willing to love me
To fully give yourself
To be willing to stick with only me
To love no one else
That is the will of love

To lay beside me
To not say anything aloud
To become one with me
To do wonderful things to make me smile
That is the will of love

To be willing to cry with me
To never want to lie to me
To be willing to get down on one knee
To say those four magical words
"Will you marry me?"
To me, that is the true will of love

DEAR DADDY

Dear daddy
I thank you for being
A part of my life
I thank-you for caring
For me so much
I thank –you for no matter
Where you stayed
I thank-you for always
Keeping in touch
I thank-you for the pep talks
And always wanting me to be the best
I thank-you for continuing
To love me even when I made you stressed
I thank-you for always taking me
Around your family
I thank-you
For not being ashamed of me
I thank-you for always encouraging
And supporting me
And I thank-you for just
Simply loving me
I thank-you for playing your part
As being my daddy

       Love always
       Boosie

MY SISTER, MY FRIEND

My sister, my friend,
As it comes close to being a year
Dealing with the memory of your death
All over again, I fear.

So many things you and your babies
Didn't get to do
And as I sit here trying to fight back my tears
I'm still missing you.

My sister, my friend,
I hold the fondest memory of you
And the kids dear to my heart

I knew way back when
The first time we met
So many years ago,
Even though we were like day and night,
Our friendship would never grow apart.

At times I have to remind myself
That you're in a better place
And no matter what has happened
Our friendship,
Our bond,
Our love,
Can never be taken away.

My sister, my friend,
Forgive me while it's hard to
Make this particular poem long,
I admit to you that sometimes
My emotions get the best of me
Then it gets really hard for me to remain strong.

My sister, my friend,
I love you forever
As only a good friend can,
Forever and always
Until the next life
When we meet again.

                    RIP
                    Lisa (leevis) Shelton

ONE MOTHER

Never seeing eye to eye
Not getting alone, not even trying
I step to you like no child should
But the hurtful things you say
I'm not meaning to disappoint you, just trying to
    be understood
I say I'm leaving, but make an excuse to come
    back
I need you, I hate you, and I'm hurting you
I need to be heard, there is so much I want to say
Cause in my heart I know that I'm wrong, but can
    you tell me
When will the drama stop?
You see, because I know you only get one mother

Need more time to see this thing through,
I love you to the fullest and I just don't know what
    to do.
I know it says in the Bible to obey and respect
    your mother,
But please tell me that somewhere in there,
It says for you to respect me and just give me love
    and support?
You see, because I know you only get one mother

Others on the outside looking in, tell them what
    you want to,
But they don't know where our aching history
    begins

Ignore me, deny me, but remember that I'll
    always know,
So for now I want out until the pain slows;
With no more fighting and no more swearing
Then we can sit down and really talk.
You see, because I know you only get one mother

You say I'll miss you when you're gone
That still doesn't excuse that you are sometimes
    wrong
I'm stuck in the past, moving kind of fast, trying
    to be tuff
When all I really need from you is a hug
I need for us to let go, to be mother and daughter
I need for our love to start to grow
Momma I hear you, but please just hear me
I'm just like you I need my momma,
And I know somewhere in your heart
A part of you, need me to.
You see, because I know you only get one mother

LAST NIGHT......

Last night
I fell in love with you
All over again
Like for the very first time

We made love to one another
Where we spiritually
Became one

Soulfully pleasing our minds
Our hearts
Our souls

Last night
You held me in your arms
As I listened
To our hearts beating
In one rhythm

Didn't care about any of our
Life worries
Just pleased with knowing
Being with you forever
In love
Made our life realities
Worth living
Last night........

FANTASIA 05

For all I feel you stand for, you're my inspiration
And as I struggle everyday to become a published
    author
I use you as my mentor
Not because of American Idol, no it's beyond that
It's because you're not holding back anything
To speak up about who you are and not be
    ashamed
To hold your head up high for what you believe in
Scared deep down you maybe, but you keep
    pushing forward
Your dreams your are achieving
Incredible is what I believe you are, straight from
    the hood and just doing you
Awesome is how I describe such a powerful voice,
    so keep moving forward
Breaking those barriers, because there are only a
    few who are willing to be genuinely true

MY GIFT: INDIA, CHELSEA, DEANDRE JR., KOBE

I cannot express the love that
I have for the four of you,
However, every word that I write down about you
Are words of truth.
If I had to do it again I wouldn't
Change anything,
My love runs through your veins deep,
You see,
We have a bond that all mothers should have
With their sons and daughters,
From your very first cry, to your endless laughter
All four of you are growing so fast
I can hardly keep up,
But through all of the struggles
All four of you have been by my side without a
 fuss
Through life you will stumble at times,
Cause we all do make mistakes
Right there by your side
I will be there to help you set the record straight
You see,
Without you there would be no me,
I keep going because of that
My life may dictates how yours might be,
So I pray that your lives be
As Christ-like as it can possibly be
To my babies, thank you
For making your father and my life so complete.

47

AN ASSURANCE OF OUR LOVE

A rub on the back of my neck
Sweet words whispered into my ear
Letting me know that you're still here
An assurance of your love

The kind of gestures between two people who are
    in love
Only through our eye contact can both of us
    discover
An assurance of our love

No missing of our special occasions
That means so much to the both of us
No accusations of wrong doings
Which means we truly have trust
An assurance of our love

Crazy in love is where we want to be
A love that lasts forever and that has to be
An assurance of both our love

No looking past me
No looking through you
Dealing with what this life dishes out to us
Handling it together is what we do
An assurance of our love

No argument to big
No love making too small
Here we both still stand through it all
An assurance of both our love

WANDA

A single mother is what you were
Raising three kids on your own
Daddy did what he could
When he could
But when he didn't come through
You managed to take care of us
Standing alone
No matter what people said about you
You held your head up and kept pressing on
Despite all the test and trials that single mothers
    go through
You still remained strong
Times got hard
And you went through what you went through
But you found your way back to us
And your love for us has always remained true
You gave up a lot for us
Yet you never complained of having any regrets
And for that
We love you mom,
Tonya
    Kenneth
        Volanda

And your love we appreciate
And through our love,
And through your grand kids
We hope that you never forget
Love always,
To Mom

I LOOK............

I look into your eyes and I see
The deep love that you have for me
I see you trying to be strong for everyone
For yourself, your family, and even society

I look beyond the frustrations to see
The good man that you have become
The lover, the friend, and beyond
Only I being your soul mate can see
Where you are coming from

I look to be able to care for you like
No one else can
To make you see that through good or bad
I'm still your woman
Standing by your side through the sunshine and
the rain

I look for guidance and encouragement
That only you can give me
No one can understand our bond
Only God, because you are my destiny
Continue to commit yourself to me
As I have to you
And the greatness of our love will forever be

I look for you to come closer and look into my eyes
To see the journey we are meant to take together
Just you and I
Look even closer and you will see
The deep love that I have for you as you have for
 me.

CAN YOU?

Can you?
Love me the way that I need it
Give yourself to me mentally,
Physically, and spiritually
Can you?
Come over and talk that talk I like
That sweet intellect
And at the end of the night
Nothing more than a hug would you expect
Can you?
Leave knowing spiritually that
My love is more valuable than any kiss
But not being near me for more
Than a second
My presence is what you miss
Can you?
Deal with all of that and have
The courage to wait on me
Cause we both know in the end
My love
Will be worth waiting
Can you?

FATHER

Father I hold my memories of you
Dear to my heart

And I know that you've been a part
Of my life and a great father
To me right from the very start

To know the kind of love you
Gave me is priceless and could
Never be replaced

Helping me grow from a sweet little infant
To the woman I am today
Full of love and grace

Everyday I think of you
And all that you've ever done for me

Respect I give to the man
That you were while in my life
And I thank-you for loving me
And never giving up on me

> Love Always
> Boosie

WHERE DID THE TIME GO?

Hey Love,
Tell me where did the time go?
So many things you thought about doing
But you let those opportunities pass you by
Now it seems you have grown older

Tell me where did the time go?
You've always had a thing for choosing A over B
Now you find yourself having regrets
On some of your life choices
Cause in your life right now
You don't think you are where you should be

Tell me where did the time go?
Your dreams have come and gone away
You know,
The ones you put off for another day
Could it have possibly been the wasting of time
On others lives
Trying to be their hero
When all alone without your direction
They would've been just fine

So tell me where did the time go?
There is time left to turn things around in your
life
You just have to be willing to make the sacrifice
Learn to take time for you

Know that you can't do everything for someone
     else
If you don't learn to be committed to you

Tell me where did the time go?
Don't put off your dreams any longer
For what do you have to lose?
Be open, be honest, be real to your spirit
Then yourself will you choose

MY SOUL

Sometimes I feel an empty space
in my soul that only God can fill
through His truth.

DEAR LORD

Dear Lord,
I feel trapped right now
Don't know what direction to go
I feel so helpless like my life is
Spinning out of control

I ask myself what direction do you
Want me to be in
To be in- line with your plan?
Please show me Dear Lord
In the way that only You can

I need to be freed from the things that
Are going on around me
Freed from relationships, friendships,
Hatred, and of course envy

So much hatred going on
That it's impossible to ignore
I ask that you take me beyond
What my eyes can physically see
Place my soul on a plan with you Lord
For my heart and soul to explore

Humble these words
As they come from my heart
Dear Lord,
Show me in which direction
Through you
Where You want me to start

"ETERNITY"

With wishful thinking comes hope
With hope comes meditation
With meditation comes prayer
With prayer comes a closer walk with God
With a closer walk with God, comes all fulfilled
    promises
With fulfilled promises comes no more worries or
    doubt
With no more worries or doubt comes true faith
With true faith comes spiritual peace
With spiritual peace comes Eternity with our
Father in Heaven.

AFTER THE STORM...

After the storm,

Lord, you are still here,
Even after all my family and friends seem to have
    disappeared.

You've protected me through it all keeping me
    safe,
Not once leaving me alone, to conquer my worst
    fears or to fall on my face.

After the storm...

Lord, you are still here,
Helping me pick-up, piece by piece, my crumbled
    life.

Not one time saying," I told you so", or I was
    wrong and you were right.

After the storm...

You tell me to hold my head up high and move on.
That in order to get past life tests, I must not hold
    on to grudges but,
Continue to love everyone.

Even despite them deserting me in my time of
    need,

He said to let go of the past and only then will my
    soul be free.

After the storm...

You continue to be with me, letting me know that
    the battle is yours,
Not mine.
To just trust in Him and he will supply all of my
    needs.

After the storm.

A MOTHER'S PRAYER

Lord show me how to raise my babies,
In what I call a ghetto haven.
Lord teach me that even in this world they can
    still be saved,
So I ask for the strength not to give up on them,
    that will last me all of my days.

Lord show me the survival kit for all of their
    wants and needs,
Without them trying to sacrifice their souls for
    greed.
Lord show me how to teach my babies to live with
    compassion and grace,
For them to have a personal relationship with
    you, and to learn when times get hard,
And how to believe in You and have faith.

Lord show them humbleness and humility to stay
    focused on You.
Lord train me to teach them to make all their life
    decisions through You.

Lord show me...

ENCOURAGEMENT

Enjoyment is what I feel
When I am with you
So this is just a little note to
Let you know that
I understand what you are
Going through
I send my encouragement to you
For the things
That you are facing within your
Life everyday
Just know that through keeping your faith
God will move from the tiniest pebble
To the highest mountain out of your way

BE WHO YOU ARE

Be who you are
Be great at what you do
By all means
Never let anyone steer you
Away from Gods' truth
Continue to love and respect yourself
Continue to know that Gods' love
Protects you everyday, in every way
Continue to know that sometimes
We fall short of perfection
Sometimes we do make mistakes
But knowing how to keep your head up
To accept failures as a mere life lesson
Only then will you truly be able to enjoy all of
    Gods' blessings

WAIT ON ME

Wait on me,
I shall supply all of your needs,
Believe that I will show you
Your purpose and great destiny
Wait on me,
Know that I will be your guide
Trust in me and I guarantee
You a new life
Wait on me,
Learn to be meek and humble to my words
I will fight all of your battles
So don't be discouraged
Wait on me,
I love you and want you to be happy
For there is nothing I can't do
To take care of your life matters
Wait on me,
I will give you all the riches and the promise land
You see, I am your Father,
And all that I ask is that you learn to keep My
    commands
And just learn to Wait on Me............

CREATIVITY

My creativity can't and shouldn't
Be closed in a box forever
My spirit won't survive
Not being able to express my passions
My thoughts,
Unleashing the brilliant talent that I was meant
To share will surely die
Don't torture my soul and
Keep it in captivity
I will only be weakened and so much would be lost
And that would affect both of our lives
As hard as it is, let my creativity free
To re-create the love,
The thoughts, and the passions we both once
    shared
To explore a spirit that will only thrive
With nothing but freedom on its side
My creativity can't and shouldn't be closed in a
    box forever...........

ONE DAY I WOKE UP, FINALLY FREE

One day I woke up finally free
Free from all the inside pain and anxiety
My mind is now flowing again
With so many stories to tell
Not being able to get my thoughts out on paper
Had me living through hell
But one day I woke up and was finally free
Free to choose to write again
To set my aching soul free
Now I've gotten the passion back
A positive attitude
A focus to move on whatever I choose to do
I will no longer dwell on my haunting past
If I'm to let this spiritual flow I have last
Cause you see,
One day I woke up and was finally free
Free to say I am in the drivers seat in full control
Doing everything it takes to follow my dreams
Never letting them die
Never letting them grow old
Believing in myself is now a part of me
Now my heart and soul is finally free
One day I woke up.........

WHO AM I?

When I look in the mirror
I find my reflection looking back at me
I look even further and ask myself
Who am I?
The reflection responds just a little bit differently
It says
I am a mother
I am a daughter
I am the lady you pass on the street
I am a cousin
I am a lover
I am the girl you take home for your mother to
    meet
I am who I am

I am a co-worker
I am a friend
I am the one who will be there to the bitter end
I am a mistress
I am a provider
And when needed to be I am a true rider
I am who I am

I am beautiful
I am sexy
I am a mess
I am gorgeous even when I am not dressed
I am who I am

I am loyalty
I am grace
I am integrity
I am the one who will put you in your place
I am who I am

I am a doctor
I am a homemaker
I am complete
I am a minister
I am a prophet
I am a writer
I am one who loves knowledge so I love to teach
I am who I am

I am a coach
I am a cheerleader
I am a nurse to the sick
I am a student
I am poor
I am also rich
I am who I am

I am all women
I am a lady
I am respect
I am one who has few regrets
I am who I am

I am courage
I am freedom
I am discreet
I am so many faces that is what makes me so
    unique
I am who I am

I am scared
I am walking not by sight but by faith
I am a child of God
I am apart of His mercy and grace
I am everything
I am you
I am her
I am magnificently created
For I am simply me

WITH CLOSED EYES

When I close my eyes
I can see it so clear
Like a sweet sound whispering in my ear
I lay awake at night staring
Eventually drifting off
To that special place
There I know I have beaten
The odds and won the race
When I close my eyes
The hard and tough roads I see no more
I am already at my destiny
With memories that can't be erased
I am then praised by my Father above
With a job well done
Now who could want and need for more?
When I close my eyes
I must simply remember
The journey it took to get here
For I now know that failure
Was not an option
But through Christ my destiny
Has been fulfilled
When I close my eyes........

"WHISPERS IN THE WIND"

I didn't even feel the wind blowing,
To busy sulking in my own misery.
When all the time it was God trying to talk to me.

He had been whispering in my ear for so long,
But I was ignoring his words.
Tried to do things my way, on my own.

So I got off the right path created by him,
        specifically for me,
I ended up making many mistakes along the way
Trying to fulfill my own destiny.

Could've avoided a lot of trouble if I had only took
        the time to hear him,
The words were so clear, yet I chose not to
        understand them.

So the next time I'm walking and the wind blows
        by,
I promise I'll take the time to listen,
And won't let his profound words pass me by.

I didn't even feel the wind blowing....

ENJOYING EVERYDAY LIFE

I will not let another day go by
That I am not enjoying my everyday life
Some things I know I will have to give up
But to be in the graces of God
Those things I shall sacrifice
No more dreaming for my personal relationship
With God because it is real
No more of my happiness through Christ
Shall I let the evil one steal
As I stand here I know my dreams
Are designed and ready to come true
No matter how many obstacles come my way
I know my Father will see me through it
There is no battle for me
That He will not fight
And for that reason alone is why I won't give up
Cause if this world gets dark on me
My faith in God will give me light
The light that will guide me through
Any darkness I must face
His truth in my mind
In my heart and in my soul
Can never be erased
I will not let another day go by
That I am not enjoying my everyday life

ABOUT THE AUTHOR

Volanda is a born native of Detroit, Michigan who has had a passion for writing since her childhood days growing up on Detroit's Eastside. So, it is no surprise that she grew up with the dream of becoming an author. *My Mind, My Heart, My Soul,* which is her first book, is a book of poetry that reflects the everyday ups and downs of her life and the lives of others who have been a part of her life's journey.

Volanda still resides in Detroit with her wonderful husband, DeAndre and their four great children, India, Chelsea, DeAndre, and Kobe Wilson. She is a member of Faith Reconciliation Tabernacle Center of Detroit under the leadership of Pastor Ray Johnson, and First Lady Leola Johnson. Volanda spends a great deal of her time reading and writing and is a member of Writers for Christ writing group where she gets a lot of love and support from its members. She is currently working on two new projects, which includes starting her own business to promote literacy to the youth of Detroit. Her future plan is to make writing a full time career.